Perkin and the Pastrycook

A Play for Children

David Foxton

A SAMUEL FRENCH ACTING EDITION

FOUNDED 1830

SAMUELFRENCH-LONDON.CO.UK
SAMUELFRENCH.COM

Copyright © 1990 by David Foxton
All Rights Reserved

PERKIN AND THE PASTRYCOOK is fully protected under the copyright laws of the British Commonwealth, including Canada, the United States of America, and all other countries of the Copyright Union. All rights, including professional and amateur stage productions, recitation, lecturing, public reading, motion picture, radio broadcasting, television and the rights of translation into foreign languages are strictly reserved.

ISBN 978-0-573-15031-9

www.samuelfrench-london.co.uk

www.samuelfrench.com

FOR AMATEUR PRODUCTION ENQUIRIES

UNITED KINGDOM AND WORLD EXCLUDING NORTH AMERICA

plays@SamuelFrench-London.co.uk

020 7255 4302/01

Each title is subject to availability from Samuel French,

depending upon country of performance.

CAUTION: Professional and amateur producers are hereby warned that *PERKIN AND THE PASTRYCOOK* is subject to a licensing fee. Publication of this play does not imply availability for performance. Both amateurs and professionals considering a production are strongly advised to apply to the appropriate agent before starting rehearsals, advertising, or booking a theatre. A licensing fee must be paid whether the title is presented for charity or gain and whether or not admission is charged.

The professional rights in this play are controlled by Samuel French Ltd, 52 Fitzroy Street, London, W1T 5JR.

No one shall make any changes in this title for the purpose of production. No part of this book may be reproduced, stored in a retrieval system, or transmitted in any form, by any means, now known or yet to be invented, including mechanical, electronic, photocopying, recording, videotaping, or otherwise, without the prior written permission of the publisher. No one shall upload this title, or part of this title, to any social media websites.

The right of David Foxton to be identified as author of this work has been asserted by him in accordance with Section 77 of the Copyright, Designs and Patents Act 1988

CHARACTERS

Wat, a pastrycook
Perkin, a royal odd-job man
Town Crier
Sly, a knave and a thief
Tinker, another knave and thief
Emperor Sigismund the Fourteenth
Empress Wilhelmina
Princess Sophie
Chief Minister
Guard Captain
Soldiers
Ladies-in-Waiting

ACT I   The Palace of Emperor Sigismund XIV in the Lands West of the Tarsus River

ACT II   The Lands East of the Tarsus River

ACT III   The Palace of Emperor Sigismund XIV

Time—sometime during the Middle Ages

ACT I

Two acting levels, one high and one low, are suggested, with access to the lower one through the audience

Wat and Perkin enter with a large box: they move through the audience and ad-lib their entrance on the following lines:

Wat Ooh! Let's have a rest, Perkin ... I'm out of breath already—just a little rest. So that I can get my strength back. (*The box is rested*) Whew!— that's better: I'm aching all over—it's too heavy, there should be more than just the two of us to move it—heavy thing—after all we're not used to this work ... well *I'm* not used to it.
Perkin Come on, let's get on with it ...
Wat Ooh! Er! It seems heavier still now. Or I'm weaker ... oof! What a weight ... ooh! What can be inside I wonder ... it feels like lead ... ooh! ... my back! ... I'm not as young as I was ... my arms are being pulled out of their sockets ... what a weight!

They reach centre stage

Ooh! Thank heavens for that. Can we leave it here.

Perkin nods

Thank goodness. And we can have another little rest ...
Perkin Oh no! Not another one ...
Wat But I need it, Perkin, I'm not strong like you. I need a rest ...
Perkin But we've another box to bring in ...
Wat Another! Oh heavens! No! ... I couldn't manage another ... my arms would snap off I feel sure.
Perkin Oh, stop complaining—let's go and get the job done.
Wat Oh it's all right for you—you're young and strong ... what about me?—I'm not suited for this work. I'm an artist, I am not a labourer.
Perkin You're a what?
Wat I'm an artist—a creator. I'm ...

Perkin laughs

And what's so funny about that, eh?
Perkin You—an artist! Oh that's the best joke yet—an artist!
Wat Well, I am.
Perkin You were a cook!
Wat I *am* a cook. An artist with food. A creator of dishes—a gourmet!
Perkin And so what are you doing here—lifting boxes with me? If you're an artist.

Wat You know very well why I'm here.
Perkin Tell me again.
Wat No, I won't.
Perkin Come on—tell us—tell us all about yourself.
Wat Stop it!
Perkin Oh no! Not now. Come on, tell us all—tell us your tale of woe ... Quiet please! Quiet everyone—pray silence please—let's all hear the story of my friend Wat, Wat the Pastrycook ...

Silence

Come on, Wat—we're all waiting—
Wat No, I shan't!
Perkin Oh! Now, now—don't sulk, tell us all your problems—
Wat No! I'm not going to now!
Perkin Come on, Wat—come on, Watty—we're all waiting—
Wat I won't!
Perkin Well then *I* will. Ladies and gentlemen! This is the story of Wat the Pastrycook—Pastrycook to the Emperor—an artist with flour and water. Now Wat worked in the Emperor's kitchen until—how long ago was it?
Wat Two weeks.
Perkin Until two weeks ago, when he was *sacked*!
Wat It wasn't fair—it wasn't my fault.
Perkin What wasn't?

Silence

Wat I'm not saying ...
Perkin He was sacked because he made some pies, but not with flour—oh no—Wat used plaster of Paris.
Wat It wasn't my fault ...
Perkin And all the pies were rock hard ...
Wat It wasn't my fault ...
Perkin And the Chief Minister broke his jaw trying to eat one ... and one fell on the Guard Captain's foot and broke his toe ... and the Empress lifted one and dislocated her shoulder ... and ...
Wat It was a plot—a plan—the Chief Cook doesn't like me—he put the plaster out where the flour was—I didn't know—it was an understandable mistake—it might have happened to anyone—it's not fair—it wasn't *my* fault!
Perkin And poor old Wat was dismissed from the kitchens and sent to work with me—the Palace's odd-job man. So now he's an odd-job man's assistant.
Wat I'm an artist—a pastrycook.
Perkin You're an odd-job man's assistant. And come on now, you've rested long enough. Let's go and get the other box—or the Emperor will dismiss us both—and then where can we go? Come on ...

Perkin exits

Wat Look Perkin—no wait a minute—I mean it really wasn't my fault—I

Act I

... I was tricked ... I was cheated—listen to me, Perkin, listen ... oh wait a minute ... oh I'm out of breath again already!—phew!

Wat exits

A knocking is heard from the inside of the box that has been left on stage. There might also be some muffled shouts. Clearly there is someone inside it

A bell is heard ringing: and a Town Crier comes through the audience, ringing his bell

Town Crier Oyez! Oyez! Oyez! (*Ringing his bell*) Oyez! Oyez! Oyez! (*Repeat until in position*) A proclamation from his noble highness Emperor Sigismund the Fourteenth, Lord of the Lands West of the Tarsus River.

Wat and Perkin enter with another box and sit on it to listen to the bulk of the proclamation

Be it known that the Emperor hereby announces to all present that the two thieves who last week persuaded His Majesty, by trickery, to wear a non-existent suit of clothes and to walk in procession through the town in his underwear have been caught. His Majesty is having them brought to the palace today where they will stand trial. It is further decreed that all references to the Emperor's New Clothes will be banned from all books and documents, and no-one is to make fun of his Majesty about this incident. Long Live the Emperor!

Town Crier exits, ringing his bell

Wat and Perkin move the box onto the acting area

Wat How about that, Perkin?
Perkin What do you mean?
Wat Well, fancy the Emperor being made a fool of, eh? Walking about in his underwear, eh?
Perkin That's right.
Wat What a laugh. I wish I'd seen it. Ho! Ho! What a sight! And all the people watching too!—My word.
Perkin Don't talk about it, you could land yourself in a lot of trouble.
Wat But it's so funny, I mean, fancy all those people watching and the Emperor just walking through them wearing just his ...
Perkin Stop it!
Wat Well, I mean ...
Perkin No more! Just be quiet. Now look. I'll just go back to the office and see if there are any more jobs for us. You stay here and guard these boxes—I believe they're very important. Nothing must happen to them—nothing at all—so look after them well—they are very valuable.

Perkin exits

Wat (*on his own: to himself and the audience*) In his underwear! Oh, my word! What a scene—what an amazing thing! How funny—I wish I'd seen it—ha! ha!—in his vest and his ... oh! ha! ha!—great heavens what a giggle ... (*He sits and chuckles to himself*)

A noise from a box: Wat stops laughing; then thinks nothing of it—he sits back chuckling: another noise

What was that? I could have sworn I heard a ... from ... no it couldn't be! From the boxes—never! And I've got to look after them. Guard them, Perkin said. My job—to look after them—what a comedown ... valuable, he said—valuable indeed! What's in them I wonder—mm? (*examines them*)—locked! Well—they must be valuable. And they're heavy—very heavy! Perhaps they've got treasure inside—gold and silver and diamonds and ... that'd be valuable. All that treasure! Phew! What a lot of money—how rich the Emperor must be ... more money than he needs. Much more. If I had half his wealth—no a quarter—a tenth—a—well just a little weeny bit I could buy my own bakery, my very own—I'd be my own employer. A pastrycook with his own shop! But I'll never have enough money—never!—not a chance—not a ... wait a minute ... I could open a box and take ... no! that'd be wrong—stealing that'd be. But I could just take a look, eh? Just to see if it was all safe and sound. A little look—(*he goes to a box and attempts to force the lock*)—no-one need know, and it won't harm the treasure, after all I ought to know what I'm guarding—now just a little more persuasion. Just a little twist and ...

The lid flies open and out jumps a man, Sly

Eeow! Help! No! Help it wasn't me—help! Perkin, help me—ooh! I didn't mean it, I didn't know I was just checking ... just seeing that ...

During all this the man unfastens the other box and another man, Tinker, joins him—they watch Wat

... everything was safe—that nothing had happened to the contents—oh Perkin! Perkin! Come back and help me, oh help me!
Sly What is your will, O master?
Wat Come on, Perkin! Come on! Oh ... pardon?
Sly I said "what is your will, O master?" We are the genies of the boxes—your will is our command.
Tinker Your will is our command, O master!
Sly Whatever you desire shall be our pleasure.
Tinker Our pleasure!
Sly Gold?
Tinker Or silver?
Sly Diamonds.
Tinker Rubies.
Sly Emeralds.
Tinker Pearls.
Sly A fortune.
Tinker Two fortunes.
Sly Three.
Tinker Or more!
Sly What is your wish?
Tinker O master!

Act I

Wat Treasure? Pleasure? For me? Genies—out of the boxes! For me? Just waiting to do what I ask?—my word! oh my goodness—wait till I tell Perkin.
Sly No! No! O . . . master! That must not be.
Tinker No! No! indeed . . . for you see we are to serve you . . . only you.
Sly No-one else. No one else must know about us . . .
Tinker No-one else must ever know about us . . .
Wat Oh, but Perkin's my friend—I couldn't not tell him.
Sly But you mustn't.
Tinker No!
Sly He mustn't know.
Tinker Not at all!
Sly In fact . . . in fact . . . O Master! Only *you* can see us—to everyone else we are invisible. Only you—our master—can see us. Perkin would not believe you . . .
Tinker Hey, that's good—I like that . . .

Sly punches Tinker

Oooh!
Sly Only you, great master, have the power to see us.
Wat Oh well! In that case things are different—you should have said before . . . I mean I can understand that . . .
Sly Now what is your will, O master?
Tinker O great and glorious master!
Wat Oh, yes—well er . . . er! Well, first of all I should like some . . . some money so that I can open a shop and then . . .
Sly Very well master, we go to do your bidding . . . remain here and count up to five hundred . . .
Tinker With your eyes closed.
Sly . . . with your eyes *tightly* closed, and we shall return with all you desire . . .
Tinker . . . as long as you don't tell Perkin about us.
Sly . . . oh yes . . . as long as you keep our secret.
Wat I shall! I shall! Not a word! I'll do it now (*he closes his eyes*) one, two, three, four (*he continues counting*)

Tinker and Sly shut the boxes, adjust the locks, shake each others hands, laugh and then sneak off

Perkin enters

Perkin Wat! . . . are you still on guard?
Wat Twenty-one, twenty-two, twenty-three . . .
Perkin Twenty-nine, twenty-two, fourteen, fifty-three, fifty-six, fifty, seventy-six . . .
Wat Oh heck, Perkin, now I've lost count . . . I'll have to start again—one, two . . .
Perkin What are you doing?
Wat Counting—seven, eight, nine . . .

Perkin What for?
Wat ... eleven, twelve, thirteen, fourteen—I'm counting—fifteen, sixteen—so that I'll be able to—seventeen, eighteen—so that ... no, I can't tell you!
Perkin You can't tell me?
Wat That's right—nineteen, twenty, twenty-one ...
Perkin What can't you tell me?
Wat Twenty-four, twenty-five—I can't tell you about the two ... oh no! You don't catch me like that—twenty-six, twenty-seven ...
Perkin Aren't you going to tell me?
Wat (*shaking his head*) ... twenty-eight, twenty-nine, thirty, thirty-one, thirty-two ...
Perkin All right!—Don't tell me then! I only hope that you've kept an eye on these boxes.

Wat stops counting

Have you?

Wat nods and continues the count

Because these are the Emperor's boxes.

Wat stops counting

And very valuable they are to him.

Wat continues counting very quickly

You haven't been meddling, have you?

Wat shakes his head and slows his counting down

I'm pleased to hear it, because the entire court is coming here any minute now.

Wat increases the speed of his counting to a tremendous pace

> There is a drum-beat or a fanfare and the Court enters—all bandaged suitably as a result of Wat's failures of pastry—Soldier (with banner), Emperor and Empress, Princess, Ladies-in-Waiting, Chief Minister and Guard Captain, and the Town Crier at the rear

Perkin moves Wat out of the way, to the side of the main acting areas

Town Crier (*ringing his bell*) Silence please for his esteemed highness, the Emperor Sigismund the Fourteenth, Lord of the Lands West of the Tarsus River.

The Emperor steps forward

Emperor Er ... Subjects. Devoted subjects. Today is an ... er ... well ... an ... er auspicious occasion. Today is a day on which I ... I ... I, your Emperor can once again hold his ... er ... er ... head up ... high—without fear of being laughed at and ... er ... ridiculed. Last week ... oh dear ... last week ... oh I don't want to talk about it ... but ... well I was made the ... the ...

Empress Laughing stock.
Emperor Er... yes... thank you, my dear..., ... the... er laughing stock of the entire country. Through the trickery of two knaves, I, your... er...
Empress Emperor.
Emperor Yes... er... your Emperor, Sigismund the... er...
Empress Fourteenth.
Emperor The... yes... the Fourteenth...
Town Crier Lord of the Lands West of the Tarsus River.
Emperor Thank you... was made to seem a fool in front of the population. I was made to... I was tricked into... into... I had to walk... to... they persuaded me to... oh dear—it's no good I can't say it—it's too embarrassing. Tell them... Chief Minister...
Chief Minister Mmmm mm (*He can't speak for his face is bandaged*)
Empress It's no good asking him, Sigismund... you know he broke his jaw on that pie that dreadful pastrycook made out of plaster instead of flour ... you should have had him beheaded like I said... foolish fellow that he is—off with his head I say.
Wat What? Oh dear... (*He loses count and has to begin again*)
Emperor Oh yes! Yes, I do remember now—poor fellow... and how is your mouth, Chief Minister?
Chief Minister Er... mm... er... ergh!
Emperor Oh dear, I'm so sorry... I do hope that you'll feel better soon...
Empress Never mind about him, Sigismund... what about the Guard Captain's foot... and my dislocated shoulder... and all the other injuries that pastrycook caused...
Emperor Dear me, yes... and how are...
Empress Not now, Sigismund—carry on with the trial.
Emperor The trial, my dear?
Empress The trial, Sigismund, the trial—the trial of the two thieves who made you walk through the streets in your vest and pants!

Shock all round

Emperor Oh dear! Oh dear! Oh I wish you hadn't said that—now I do feel silly—everyone's looking all over again. It wasn't my fault they said it was an invisible suit...
Empress And you fell for it!
Emperor We all did, my dear. You as well, I recall.
Empress Well, they were very convincing. I thought it was all true. And they were very charming men—and so handsome... they said how beautiful I was, I remember...
Emperor They told a great many lies!
Empress What!
Emperor About the clothes, I mean, my dear—about the suit.
Guard Captain But we catched them yer 'ighness.
Emperor What's that... oh yes! Captain! Yes indeed you catched... er, caught them right enough.
Guard Captain And we brung 'em 'ere for trial.

Emperor Yes, yes, that is so.
Guard Captain Then we can be'ead 'em when we find 'em guilty.
Emperor Well ... er ... yes, I suppose so.
Empress Let the trial begin.
Town Crier Oyez! Oyez! Oyez! All people who have business in the court today are asked to be silent before the Grand Judge, his esteemed Majesty the Emperor Sigismund the Fourteenth, Lord of the Lands West of the Tarsus River, on this the twenty-eighth day of November in the year fourteen hundred and ... and ...

Empress		Forty-eight.
Emperor		Forty-seven.
Chief Minister	*(together)*	Mmmmm.
Ladies-in-Waiting		Forty-nine.
Guard Captain		Forty-free!

With these ad-lib dates from the others Wat again loses count

Town Crier The court is now in session. The prisoners are charged with knavery and trickery in that on the twenty-first day of November in the year fourteen hundred and ... and ...

A number of ad-libs — Wat again loses count

... the strangers, Tinker and Sly, did persuade his Royal Highness to wear a non-existent suit of clothes and to consequently become a laughing stock among his subjects when he walked through the streets.
Empress In his vest and pants.
Emperor Oh, please my dear ... sshh!—the embarrassment!
Empress But they were clean on, Sigismund.
Emperor Even so my dear ... ssh! please! Oh dear, I'm blushing already.
Town Crier Let the prisoners stand forth!

Nothing happens

Empress Let the prisoners stand forth!
Emperor Let the prisoners stand ... f ... where are they?
Chief Minister Mm mmm!
Emperor What? Oh don't bother trying old chap ... it must be very painful.
Empress Captain of the Guard—where are the prisoners?
Guard Captain We catched 'em your 'ighness.
Empress Where are they then?
Guard Captain In order to facilitate their not gettin' away, I ordered that they were to be brung to the court in secret.
Empress Well—tell us where they are.
Guard Captain They are in those boxes—your 'ighness.
Emperor Well then—open the boxes and let them out.

Guard Captain and Soldier move to the boxes: Wat stops counting and tries to creep away—Perkin holds him

Perkin And where are you going?

Act I

Wat Er ... well, I ... er. I've just remembered I have to go to ... see ... no! I promised I would ... I ... er.
Perkin You didn't touch those boxes while I was away did you?
Wat Didn't I?
Perkin You didn't ... oh no ... don't say you tried to look inside ... that you ... oh no!

The boxes are opened

Emperor There's no-one there!
Empress Empty!
Chief Minister Mmmmm!
Guard Captain They've got away, Your Majesty!
Emperor Away? Escaped!
Empress By heavens someone will pay for this! Who brought the boxes here? Who was the carrier? Who was in charge?
Perkin I was, Your Highness.
Empress Name?
Perkin Perkin, Your Majesty, court odd-job man.
Empress You couldn't bring them on your own—who helped you?
Perkin Er.
Empress Speak now! Who was your assistant?

Wat turns and puts up his hand

You again! Sigismund see who it is? That dreadful pastrycook, that maker of rock-hard pies—didn't I say he would cause more trouble—what is your name?
Wat That's right ma'am.
Empress I said "what is your name?"
Wat It is, Your Majesty.
Empress How many times must I ask ...
Perkin Excuse me ma'am. If I might explain—his name is Wat.
Empress What?
Perkin WAT!
Wat Yes?
Perkin No!
Empress Enough of this. It doesn't matter what his name is.
Wat That's right.
Empress Quiet, fool! You've caused sufficient trouble in this court— Sigismund!—pronounce judgement—he let your prisoners escape.
Emperor Did you?
Wat It was an accident—a mistake—I didn't know they were there my lord—I ...
Emperor Oh well, I see in that case I think ...
Empress Off with his head!

Guard Captain draws his sword: Wat is forced to his knees

Wat Oh no! Oh help! Oh Perkin—please—I ... oh ...
Perkin Your Majesties! ... Do not do this I beg of you. Wat has done

wrong—but he is no more guilty than I am. I should not have left him alone to guard such valuable boxes. He was not to know what they contained. And if he opened them it would only be natural curiosity—and who does not suffer from a certain amount of natural curiosity? Once the boxes were open, poor Wat here obviously was tricked by the prisoners—just as I would have been tricked, Your Highness. Just as you were tricked yourself, Your Majesty. Please, please give him one more chance I beg you.

Empress Nonsense! Off with both their heads!

Emperor No! Wait! ... I am ... er ... Emperor here. I know at times how easy it is to be tricked. I will give him one more chance—but this time he really must prove himself with it—he must recapture the prisoners within three days. If he does that, all is forgiven and he can even take up his former position in the Royal Kitchens. If not, my soldiers and huntsmen will be given orders to track him down and to bring him back for punishment.

The Empress makes to protest

That is my judgment.

Town Crier Long live the Emperor!

Wat (*Rising to his feet*) Oh, Your Majesty, how can I thank you enough, I (*in rising to his feet he manages to step on the Guard Captain's bandaged foot, to trap the Soldier's hand in the box, to nudge the Empress's bad arm, etc.*) Oh sorry! Oh sorry! Sorry!

The Court retires—all protesting loudly to the Emperor or talking about the situation

Town Crier (*as he moves through the audience*) Oyez! Oyez! Oyez! Wat the Pastrycook has three days in which to recapture the two prisoners who escaped from the Palace courtyard this afternoon. Failure to do this will cause him to lose his head and forfeit all his lands and processions. Long live the Emperor, Sigismund the Fourteenth, Lord of the Lands West of the Tarsus River. Oyez! Oyez! Oyez!

Town Crier exits

Wat apologises profusely through all this—Perkin has watched it all happen and now sits or leans and mops his brow

Wat Phew! Oh my word! Oh my word! We showed them then, Perkin!

Perkin Did we?

Wat I thought I was a dead one there—I really did! And now I have the chance of my old job back again.

Perkin When you recapture the thieves.

Wat Well yes, I know, but that won't take us long.

Perkin Us?

Wat Yes, us. You will help me won't you, Perkin? I mean without you I can't possibly manage it. Where would I be now without you? Eh? I mean you spoke up for me didn't you?

Act I

Perkin And landed myself in a real load of trouble as a result.
Wat Ah, but with two of us, we'll soon be able to recapture them—won't we?

Silence

I mean two heads are better than one—aren't they?

Silence

What shall we do first, Perkin?
Perkin Ssh! I'm thinking.
Wat Oh!

He strolls about, looking around—he opens one of the boxes and peers in, looking all round it

Perkin I believe those two thieves may have come from the East, beyond the Tarsus River—perhaps we ought to look there.
Wat Oh no! Not there! It's a dreadful place—I've heard about it—there's dragons and thieves and—Oh no! Perkin not there!—Please not there!
Perkin Do you want to stay here and lose your head?
Wat No! Great heavens no!
Perkin And so we'll have to go across the river.
Wat If you say so.
Perkin Now, we'll need food and weapons for such a journey.

A maid, Princess Sophie in disguise, enters from the Palace carrying swords and bundles of food

Sophie Here Perkin, Wat—these should be all you need.
Perkin Swords, food—it *is* all we need. But who are you?
Sophie I work in the kitchens, I heard the story of the trial from one of the ladies-in-waiting—I thought you would need weapons and supplies—so I packed up the food and "borrowed" the swords from the Guard Captain's armoury.
Perkin Well done! Don't you think so, Wat?
Wat I don't remember her in the kitchens.
Sophie No—you wouldn't. I'm ... er ... new there.
Perkin That's why you don't remember her—come on, pick up your supplies and your sword.
Wat Perhaps it's a trap.
Perkin How could it be? Come on—take your bundle of food.
Wat I've got it here.
Perkin Well, then whose is this one?
Sophie Mine!
Perkin }
Wat } (*together*) Yours!
Sophie Yes, I'm coming with you.
Perkin With us!
Wat I told you it was a trap.
Perkin It might be dangerous.

Sophie I don't care.
Wat I don't think she should come—two's enough.
Perkin I thought you said two heads were better than one.
Wat I did!
Perkin Well, aren't three heads better than two?
Wat Oh yes! I suppose they are, I never thought of that.
Perkin Come on then—let's waste no more time: we'll journey to the Tarsus River and then cross into the lands to the East.

They move out: Wat is slow

Wat Oh not too fast you two. I'll be out of breath before we reach the highroad. Oh do slow down a bit. Phew! Wait!

Perkin, Wat and Sophie exit

Noise from the Palace. Alarm bells and shouting. All the Court rushes on, the Emperor in dressing gown

Emperor Now what is it? What is it? I was just going to change for dinner. What is the matter?
Empress It's the princess.
Emperor What is?
Empress She has gone! She has run away!
Emperor Run away! Er ... how do you know?
Empress She left this note for me. It says "I have left the palace to help recapture the thieves—back in three days' time: love Sophie."
Emperor What a nice thought that—to help recapture the ... she's gone where!
Empress At last you're seeing sense. She's run off—run off with that pastrycook and that Perkin to try to capture those two tricksters. Anything might happen to her!
Emperor You're right. They won't get away with this. It's almost kidnapping! Wait till I get my ... er ... er ... hands on those two, and the other two—I'll give them tricks. Call out the ... er ... guard! Give me a sword.

(*Guard Captain does*)

There's no time to be lost. Let's get after them now! Come guard, come Captain, away we go!

He takes off dressing gown and runs down hall waving sword—in his vest and pants. Laughter. He realises his mistake

Oh dear ... I mean ... oh ... please don't look ... I ... oh ... well ... don't laugh ... please ... oh the embarrassment ... oh my word ... again!

He retires to the Palace, ad-libbing, the Court laughs at him

ACT II

The Town Crier appears in the centre of the theatre, ringing his bell

Town Crier Oyez! Oyez! Oyez! (*Ringing his bell*) Oyez! Oyez! Oyez! Be it hereby known that his Royal Highness the Emperor Sigismund the Fourteenth, Lord of the Lands West of the Tarsus River, offers a reward of five thousand shillinks to anyone giving information that might lead to the capture of the palace odd-job man, Perkin, and Wat, one-time pastrycook to the Court. A warrant for their arrest on a charge of abducting the Princess Sophie has been issued today. These men may be dangerous and no-one should attempt to capture them since they could be armed. They were last seen heading for the lands East of the Tarsus River. (*He rings his bell*) Long Live the Emperor!

He moves on to another place and we might hear his bell and part of the proclamation from this other place.

Meantime the scene has been altered to show the lands East of the Tarsus

Perkin and Sophie enter: they have crossed the river

Perkin We can rest here, for a while

Sophie sits

Though I don't think we should wait for too long. No-one ever feels safe in these parts. You're not nervous are you?
Sophie What? Me? Oh no, no—I'm not at all nervous.
Perkin That's good at least. There have been such mysterious stories about this area.
Sophie There have?
Perkin (*sitting next to her*) Oh yes—my word yes. About witches and hobgoblins and dragons and ... you're sure you're not nervous at all?
Sophie No! no! ... not at all ... (*She moves closer to him*).
Perkin ... and trolls and wizards too of course ... they roam around these lands ... moaning ... and wailing ...

Moans and wails off. Sophie grabs Perkin and Perkin grabs Sophie

Perkin
Sophie } (*together*) What was that?

They part

Perkin I thought you weren't nervous!

Sophie You're as nervous as I am!
Perkin
Sophie } (*together*) Nonsense.

They turn away from each other. Moans and wails off again. Sophie and Perkin grab each other again

Perkin We mustn't be frightened.
Sophie But I am.

Moans and wails off

Sophie It's coming closer.
Perkin I'll look after you.

Moans and wails

Perkin Quick let's hide over there. Come on . . .

They hide at one side of the acting area. The moans and wails grow . . . and Wat enters, he has obviously had difficulty crossing the river—he is wet, his boots hang round his neck, he is carrying the weapons and provisions

Wat Ooh! Aaah! Urggh! Groo! Oh! Oh! Oh! Oh! . . . my word . . . oh . . . Perkin . . . oh where are you?˙ . . . oh I'm wet and tired . . . oh . . . why didn't you wait for me at the bridge? . . . oh . . . oh . . . I'll bet they didn't almost drown . . . I'll bet they didn't fall in the river . . . oh, I must sit down . . . and rest and get dry . . . (*He sits*)

Perkin and Sophie emerge from hiding during this speech

. . . I wish I hadn't come . . . I'm frightened enough . . . nasty place . . . dragons and beasties and things that go bump in the . . .
Perkin (*in a deep voice*) So there you are!

Wat jumps

Wat Oh spare me (*down on his knees*), spare me your dragonship, your honour, your . . .
Perkin Get up, Wat! It's us!
Wat I meant no harm your greatness, I . . . (*it dawns*) . . . Perkin! I'll never forgive you—first you leave me carrying all the equipment, then you leave me to fall in the Tarsus River, and then you frighten me to death . . . almost.
Perkin But not quite, Wat! Not quite! Now listen, we're going to rest here a while, have a meal then carry on and hope to catch up with the two thieves by about lunchtime tomorrow . . . so what we'll do first is . . .
Wat Get dry!
Perkin No! . . . I mean yes—in your case anyway, Wat—look you'll find some dry clothes in my pack, you change, I'll find some wood to make a fire . . . and you . . . I don't know your name . . .
Sophie Er . . . Soph . . . er . . . Gretel . . .
Perkin You . . . Gretel, you can unpack the food, ready for some supper . . .
Sophie For some what?

Act II

Perkin Supper ... surely you made supper in the palace kitchens?
Sophie In the palace kitchens? ... Oh yes! In the palace kitchens, oh yes, they did ... I mean I did ...
Perkin Well, get on with it then ... found something Wat?

Wat nods as he pulls clothes from the pack

Well, change quickly then give Gretel a hand.

Perkin exits right

Wat and Sophie smile at each other

Sophie I'll ... er ... prepare some supper then ...
Wat Oh yes.

They smile at each other again

Wat I'll change my clothes then ...
Sophie Oh yes.

Wat makes as if to remove his trousers

Sophie Oh!

Wat jumps

Wat What! ... where?
Sophie You're not going to change right here are you?
Wat Aren't I?
Sophie Well ... I mean it would be rather embarrassing ... wouldn't it?
Wat Oh it's all right ... I don't mind.
Sophie But *I* do ... couldn't you change somewhere else?
Wat Well, I suppose I could go over there and change ...
Sophie Thank you so much.
Wat Though you're the first palace kitchen maid who ever objected. (*He picks up his boots*) Ow!
Sophie What's the matter?
Wat There's something in my boot.
Sophie Where?
Wat There! (*He shakes a large fish out*) ... how about that? My luck must be changing ... we'll be able to have a really good supper ... I'll go and change ... you gut and clean the fish, chop its head off (*he hands it to her*) ... all ready for ... you've done it before haven't you?
Sophie Oh ... yes ... many times!
Wat Are you sure you work in the Palace kitchens?
Sophie Of course I'm sure.
Wat I've never seen you there.
Sophie I'm new, remember ... you'd been dismissed when I came ...
Wat Oh ... well! You get on with it ... I'll go and change.

Wat exits left

During this speech the thieves, Sly and Tinker, appear behind Sophie. They listen and size up the situation, then they disguise themselves in large cloaks and add false beards. They move in left and right from rear—"collecting herbs"

Sophie (*dropping the fish*) ... oh dear, now what shall I do? I can't possibly prepare a fish, I don't know where to begin ... and Perkin will be back soon ... I'll just have to tell them the truth, tell them who I am. Wait a minute though, where's the food I gave them ... (*She finds it*) ... wet through! Wat was carrying it when he fell in the river.... oh well ... I'll have to tell them now. There's no way out. (*She sits disconsolately*)
Sly A little bit of marjoram ...
Tinker A sprig of thyme ...
Sly Some sprays of mint.
Tinker A bunch of fennel.
Sly But not dock (*he discards it*).
Tinker Or dandelion (*he disgards it*).
Sly Nor chickweed (*he discards it*).
Tinker Nor groundsel (*he discards it*)

They are now together centre front: Sophie has watched them and risen

Sophie Excuse me.
Sly
Tinker } (*together*) Who was that?
Sophie It's me ... over here.

Sly and Tinker continue collecting herbs rapidly

Sly Rosemary.
Sophie No ... my name's Gretel ...
Tinker Bay Leaf.
Sly Sage.
Tinker ... and onion.

Sly nudges Tinker

Sophie Excuse me ... please.
Sly Good heavens.
Tinker Good heavens, indeed.
Sly Look who it is?
Tinker Who is it?
Sophie I wonder if you could help me?
Sly Haven't we seen you somewhere before?
Sophie I don't believe so.
Tinker Are you sure?
Sly Quite sure?
Tinker We get around you know ...
Sly Selling herbs ...
Tinker ... and other things ...

Sly nudges Tinker viciously

Act II

Sophie I still don't think we've met before.
Sly Perhaps you bought some flavourings from us.
Tinker Allspice.
Sly Cinnamon.
Tinker Liquorice allsorts.
Sly (*viciously nudging Tinker*) ... all sorts of herbs and flavourings.
Sophie No, I don't think so ... in fact I'm sure.
Sly What!—never used our herbs?
Tinker Hand-picked.
Sly The very best.
Tinker None better.
Sly How do you manage to cook without them?
Sophie Well ... I don't do much cooking ...
Sly What do you do?
Sophie I'm a kitchen maid ...
Tinker And you don't do much cooking?
Sly How can that be?
Sophie I ... er ... well ... I ... I'm new ...
Sly
Tinker } (*together*) Aah!
Sly Now we understand.
Tinker We do?
Sly (*nudging Tinker*) We do.—You're a *new* kitchen maid.
Sophie In Emperor Sigismund the Fourteenth's palace kitchen.
Tinker What? (*He jumps—afraid*)
Sly Where?
Tinker When?
Sophie A palace kitchen maid, the other side of the Tarsus River, just recently.
Sly
Tinker } (*together*) Aah!
Sophie And now I have to cook this fish—and I'm afraid I don't know where to begin.
Sly
Tinker } (*together*) Aah!
Sophie Perhaps you two with your obvious knowledge of cooking could help me ... please.
Sly
Tinker } (*together*) Aah!
Sly I'm sure we can help.
Tinker Just sit down here—my dear.

They help her back and sit her down

Sly Oh, what delicate hands.
Tinker Not really a kitchen maid's at all.
Sly More like ...
Tinker Far more like ...
Sly A princess.

Sophie Oh!
Sly But what would a princess be doing here?
Tinker In the lands East of the Tarsus?
Sly Trying to cook fish ...
Tinker ... so you *must* be a kitchen maid.
Sly ... and we're here to help you with the fish.
Sophie (*rather frightened*) ... if you can spare the time ...
Sly (*drawing a knife*) But of course ...
Tinker (*drawing a knife*) ... of course ...

During the next few speeches Sly and Tinker threaten Sophie as they talk of preparing the fish

Sly Now when you've caught your fish ...
Tinker Bang it on the head ... really hard.
Sly To kill it.
Tinker Then cut off its fins—cleanly.
Sly Slice off its tail.
Tinker And then very carefully ...
Sly ... very, very carefully ...
Tinker ... and slowly ...
Sly ... cut off its head ...

They advance on her

There is a scream offstage

Sophie faints—Sly and Tinker jump back

Wat enters, carrying his boots

Wat Ooh ... ah ... I ... what a shock! ... I was putting my boots on when look what I found ... an eel (*he draws it out of his boot and waves it about—then throws it offstage*) ... a fish in one boot and an eel in the other ... have you prepared it yet, Gretel? I said have you ... (*he sees her and goes to her*) Oh, now what has happened. Oh speak to me—say something, ... say something ...
Sly She's fainted.
Wat (*to Sophie*) Pardon?
Tinker She's fainted.
Wat Is that all? Thank goodness, I thought she might have ... who are you?
Tinker We're ... we're ...
Sly Travellers.
Tinker That's it, we're travellers—passing by.
Sly We found your friend ... er ... Gretel, is it?
Wat That's right.
Tinker And you're Hansel?
Wat No I'm Wat—the pastrycook ...
Sly Ah yes!
Tinker Yes?
Sly Yes ... indeed yes ... and you have a lucky face ...

Act II

Tinker Very lucky.
Wat I do?
Sly Most certainly.
Wat Well, it's kind of you to say so.
Sly Your face could be your—fortune.
Tinker All the money you might need.
Sly To open a shop of your own—perhaps?
Wat Now it's funny you should say that . . . only the other day two . . . oh no I can't tell you.
Sly Someone like you deserves a fortune.
Tinker Indeed yes.
Sly If anyone ever tells you how to make a fortune—you should do it—immediately.
Tinker Immediately.
Wat You think I should.
Sly }
Tinker } (*together*) Indubitably!
Wat In that case . . . would you mind just looking after my friend, Gretel, here a moment? I won't be long.

He moves forward right, closes his eyes and begins counting. Sly and Tinker watch him, laugh together, then move to Sophie

Sophie (*coming round*) Wat?

Wat continues counting. Sly and Tinker grab Sophie and gag her

  Sly and Tinker exit carrying Sophie and Wat's boots

Wat (*continues loudly*) Twenty-seven, twenty-eight, twenty-nine, thirty, thirty-one, thirty two (*and so on, or whatever he is up to as the action is played*).

  Perkin enters through the auditorium

Perkin Wat! Wat! . . . Gretel! Have you made the supper? . . . here's the wood for a fire . . . Wat! (*he continues with ad-lib until the acting area is reached*) Gretel! . . . Where are you? (*He goes up to Wat*) . . . and just what are you doing now?

Wat continues counting

  Never mind about the counting—where's Gretel gone to?

Wat continues counting

  For goodness' sake, Wat. Stop counting I say! Stop! (*He shouts in Wat's ear*) STOP!

Wat continues counting

  Very well, you asked for it. (*He treads heavily on Wat's foot*)
Wat Ow!! (*He hops around holding his foot*)
Perkin Now where is Gretel?

Wat Over there! Ow! Ow! She's only fainted.

Perkin looks "over there"

Perkin Never mind fainted—she's disappeared.
Wat No, Perkin—she's fainted. I came back from changing my clothes and she had fainted just there!—my goodness, great pork pies—she has disappeared. Now that is odd.
Perkin It's more than odd. It's dangerous, where could she have gone to,— if she'd fainted someone would have had to carry her away from here ...
Wat Yes, that's right. That's what happened.
Perkin There would have to be someone else about—just a minute, what do you mean by saying "that's what happened"?
Wat Well, the two others must have taken her away.
Perkin Two others? What two others?
Wat The two men who were here when I came back.
Perkin Two men?
Wat That's right. They were looking after Gretel while I was ... counting!
Perkin You fool! You great fool! You maker of soggy pastry, you great flour fool ... do you know who those men were?
Wat No ... I don't think I'd seen them before ...
Perkin Well, listen to me and listen carefully because you have now been made a fool of *twice* by the thieves who tricked the Emperor.
Wat You mean those two men were ...
Perkin ... the two thieves you let escape earlier. The two men who we've come here to recapture. The two men who have now captured Gretel.
Wat Great currant buns! What shall we do now ... ?
Perkin We? We! Why is it that when you get us into a mess it is always "we" who have to get us out of it?
Wat I rely on you, Perkin.
Perkin I wish I didn't rely on you, Wat. Come on—take your sword, let's see if we can pick up their trail ... come on ... they could have gone any way ...

Perkin exits

Wat Yes, yes, coming Perkin ... I'll just put my boots on and ... here, now where did I ... I could have sworn I put my boots ... perhaps I put them over here ... no ... (*he searches around*) ... be with you in a minute, Perkin ... I'll just find my boots ... (*he acts out his last entrance*) ... now let me think, I'd been over there to change, because she didn't want me to change in front of her ... then I came back ... no ... I found the fish in my boot ... then she took the fish ... I changed and came back ... and she was there with the two men ... I came over ... and ... tried to bring her round ... I put my boots here ... or was it here? Then they said ... about the fortune ... and ... I walked here and counted ... and ... then Perkin came in ... and ... I wonder if *they* pinched *my* boots.

Sly and Tinker enter

Act II

They follow Wat about trying to capture him, they miss on about three occasions as he moves out of their way, but at last they capture him, gag him and march him off

Sly Of course we did.
Tinker And now *your* boots are pinching *me*!—Hey that was a joke, Sly... his boots are pinching me! Ho! Ho!
Sly Oh come on, come on, never mind the jokes.
Tinker (*explaining further*) You see *I* pinched his boots and when I tried them on they were tight, so now they're pinching me... what a laugh! And they're also wet too. I wonder how that happened? And they smell of fish. How do you think that happened, Sly?

All this as Sly and Tinker exit with Wat

Ringing of a bell offstage: the Town Crier is heard approaching

Town Crier enters

Town Crier Oyez! Oyez! Oyez! Make way for His Majesty the Emperor Sigismund the Fourteenth, Lord of the Lands West of the Tarsus River. (*He rings his bell*) Long Live the Emperor!

He may repeat this as the Court enters. The Emperor is in his underwear and wrapped in a blanket; Two soldiers carry a pike draped with the Emperor's wet clothes; the Guard Captain; the Chief Minister; the Town Crier, and possibly one or two more Soldiers—all camouflaged by pieces of greenery. Their appearance is ludicrous

Town Crier Oyez! Oyez! Oyez!...
Emperor Oh no! Please... er... not again. I don't think I could stand it. I mean you're very good... as a Crier... but please... er... no more...

Town Crier takes out his handkerchief and blows his nose—he is disheartened.

I mean... oh, don't cry... I meant... no more... at the moment... eh? I don't want to upset you... there... there... I'll tell you when... (*He gives a friendly pat on the Town Crier's shoulders. To the Guard Captain*) I do think we should perhaps try to keep him quieter... Captain... don't you agree... I mean we don't want to advertise our presence do we?
Guard Captain Your Majesty?
Emperor I mean we don't want to let everyone know we're here... do we?
Guard Captain No Your Majesty—it's a secret—Ssh!

All repeat the 'Ssh!' to each other

Emperor (*whispering*) So that's why we need to keep as quiet as possible...
Guard Captain (*nodding*) Oh yes, Your Majesty!
Emperor So let's keep him quiet eh?

The Emperor points at the Town Crier—who rings his bell. Everyone "sshs" him

No... no... not now, old chap. Sorry... so sorry!

Town Crier sulks

Oh dear! Are my clothes dry yet?

The Soldiers feel them

Soldiers Not yet, Your Highness.
Emperor I don't understand why I was the only one who fell into the river ... it's not fair—how did you manage to avoid it, Chief Minister?
Chief Minister Mmmnnmmnnnnn!
Emperor Oh, I'd forgotten about your jaw ... I do hope it's getting better ...
Chief Minister Mmmnnmm!
Emperor Splendid! ... splendid! ... Captain.
Guard Captain Your 'ighness!
Emperor Er ... just ... I mean if you don't mind my asking ... but how did I manage to fall in the river?
Guard Captain (*with military gestures*) Well, we was deploying to the left and right see ... and makin' sure that all was clear to advance ... and you ...
Emperor Yes ... yes ...
Guard Captain Well, your 'ighness, we moved forward as a trained body of men, suitably camouflaged for the terrain, when we came to the river where we thought there was a bridge ...
Emperor Yes ... and then.
Guard Captain Well, there wasn't your greatness, and you fell in ... and we 'ad to fish you out.
Emperor I remember that bit very clearly ... and now what?
Guard Captain Well sire, when your cloves is dried you can put 'em back on again ... make a fire you two ...
Emperor No! No! ... I don't really mean that, I meant where do we go from here ... how ... how can we catch up with that fellow Perkin and that confounded pastrycook ... how do we know where to look ... er ... where are we anyway? Have we by any chance brought a map with us?
Guard Captain A map? ... A map? ... (*It dawns on him*) Ah, yes a map! Right then ... who's got the map?

An argument develops between the Soldiers and the Guard Captain as to who had the map last, who gave it to whom and where it might be now. At the height of the quarrel the Town Crier produces it

Oh ... thanks ... yes thanks. 'Ere it is your 'ighness.

It is large: it is unrolled—upside down and spread out

Emperor Oh good! Now Captain do you ... er ... think you could show me where we are.

Everyone crowds round the map

Guard Captain Well now, sire, we are in fact ... er ... 'ere! (*He points out the place*)
Town Crier No! No! We're here, Your Grace! (*He points*)

Act II

Soldier I ⎫ (*together, but all* ⎧ Here!
Soldier II ⎬ *pointing differently*) ⎨ About there I reckon.
Chief Minister ⎭ ⎩ Mmmnmmm!

An argument develops. The Emperor rings the Town Crier's bell. Silence

Emperor Now ... wait a moment everyone ... er ... I've just spotted something ... now look (*he turns the map the right way round*). Now ... where do you say we are?

Everyone looks bemused and puzzled: shrugs and head-scratching, head shaking all round

... Captain would you care to point out the ... er ... place ...
Guard Captain Oh yes, sire, well, I should hazard an estimate ...
Town Crier A guess.
Guard Captain A military estimate! That we're about ... er ... here. (*He points out the spot*)

All others "tut-tut" shake their heads, cover their eyes

No! No! I'm wrong sire! I'm wrong. I meant to say about ... there. (*He points again*)

Again the others "tut-tut", shake heads, etc.— with more conviction than ever

Emperor Indeed? ... oh dear ... oh dearie dear ... oh dear me ...

All gather round him

I do hope you might be wrong about that particular spot, because it says on the map "Here be dragons".

All but the Emperor panic

Still it's most unlikely that we are at that spot, and who believes in dragons anyway.

Relief all round: some agreement

Guard Captain You're right, your 'ighness—dragons indeed! Why there are no such things, dragons—pah! We'd be a match for them any day. Dragons—pooh! Why I'd like to come face to face with just one of them monsters, I'd show it a thing or two, nasty vicious creatures—they would be *if* they existed—"Here be dragons" indeed. Who do they think they're fooling. Dragons—rubbish!

A dragon is heard

'Ere—what was that?
Emperor A dragon perhaps? (*He looks at the map*)

The dragon appears at the far end of the hall/theatre and advances towards the acting area. It is yet another disguise for Sly and Tinker who are inside it, the other four legs being Wat and Sophie. It is seen first of all by the Chief Minister—who can't tell anyone of course ...

Chief Minister (*to Guard Captain and Town Crier, pointing*) Mmmnmmm! (*He tries valiantly—with no success. He goes to the Soldiers—pointing*) Mmmnnmmmm!
Soldier I We're doing our best.
Soldier II We'll 'ave a fire goin' soon ...

The Chief Minister leaves them and goes to the Emperor

Soldier I What did he say?
Soldier II I dunno—never could understand a word he said ...
Chief Minister (*to Emperor*) Mmnnmmmm!
Emperor What's that?—Oh it's you, Chief Minister—and how's your jaw? (*He returns to the map*)
Chief Minister Mmmmmnnn!
Emperor Yes, it must be—I do sympathize ...

The Chief Minister returns to the Guard Captain and Town Crier

Chief Minister (*pointing at advancing dragon*) Mmmmmnnn!
Guard Captain Oh do leave us alone! You know we can't understand a word you ... (*he turns and sees the dragon*). Help! ... Help. It's the ... it's a ... to arms men! It's a ... Rally to me ...

The Soldiers panic and run and hide—as does the Town Crier and also the Chief Minister. The Emperor is oblivious to it all

Come back here ... we'll stand shoulder to shoulder ... to your captain, men ... one for all and ... aw! Don't leave me on my own ... come on play fair ... come on ... well wait for me then!

He runs too. The Emperor is left alone on his knees studying the map

Emperor (*rising*) There's another point I don't quite understand, Captain—about this map (*he moves to where the Captain was, his back to the dragon*) ... now where's he gone to. I could have sworn he was here ... (*he turns round face to face with the dragon*) Aargh!

The Emperor runs away—chased by the dragon—a chase around the acting area and as much of the auditorium as can be included

Help! Call out the guard ... get away you brute ... leave me alone ... help ... Guard Captain! ... help! ... oh help! don't eat me—please ... help! help! ... help! (*He finds sanctuary.*)

Perkin enters

Emperor Help!
Perkin Wat! Gretel! Where are you?

The dragon roars

Oh no! ... Get back you gruesome creature ... *He brandishes his sword* You may have eaten my friends—but you shan't have me ...

Dragon roars

Act II

I'll revenge my friends Wat and Gretel.

A fight between the dragon and Perkin ensues. Gradually, during the fight, those who have hidden come out of hiding and cheer on Perkin—encouraging the audience to do the same—by their example rather than by exhortation. During the fight Perkin loses his sword, and has to rely on dodging the dragon and punching it. Eventually he begins taking items of the Emperor's clothes and using them against the dragon—viz. throwing a cloak over its head—and then tying its legs together in two's so that it can't move, thus he has it hobbled. Success! Applause from the Court audience

Emperor (*coming forward*) Oh, well done—very well done ... you've undoubtedly saved all our lives ... well done young ... er ... er ...
Perkin Perkin.
Emperor Yes ... Well done ... er ... Perkin.
Chief Minister Mmmnmm! (Well done!)
Guard Captain Exactly the same tactics I would have used meself ...

The Soldiers laugh

That's enough of that now—tidy up over there—go on—get a move on!

The acting area is tidied up

Emperor I'll make a pronouncement. (*He makes a sign to the Town Crier*)
Town Crier (*ringing his bell*) Oyez! Oyez! Oyez! Silence please for His Majesty Emperor Sigismund the Fourteenth, Lord of the Lands West of the Tarsus River. (*He rings the bell*)
Emperor Er ... now ... er ... where shall I begin? ... er ...
Wat
Sophie } (*together, from inside the dragon*) Help! Help!
Emperor I feel that I should ... er ... should ... er ...
Wat
Sophie } (*together*) Help! Help! Let us out!
Emperor Where's that coming from?
Perkin The inside of the dragon, Your Majesty.
Emperor See what it is, Guard Captain.

He goes to do so, but the dragon roars and he leaps back

Perkin Let me.
Wat
Sophie } (*together*) Help! Help! Let us out! Let us out!

Perkin succeeds in letting them out. He unhobbles Sophie, but not Wat who falls on his face at his first move

Perkin Gretel!
Sophie Oh thank you, Perkin!

They kiss

Emperor Sophie!
Perkin Sophie?

Sophie Father! What are you doing here?
Emperor Searching for you of course.
Perkin Gretel! ... You told us your name was Gretel! ... Are you really the Princess after all ... ?
Sophie Yes, I am, Perkin—I'm sorry to have tricked you. I wanted some adventure, so I pretended to be a kitchen maid so that I could travel with you and Wat—do you forgive me?
Perkin (*kneeling*) Of course, ... Your Highness.
Emperor (*taking Perkin's sword*) And may I show my ... er ... thanks to you now for rescuing my daughter—and—saving my life. (*He dubs him*) Rise, Sir Perkin, Knight of the Lands East of the Tarsus River!

Applause

Guard Captain Your Majesty! Your Majesty!
Emperor What is it?
Guard Captain The other four legs of the dragon.
Emperor What about them?
Guard Captain Well, we've just been lookin', and they belong to the two thieves who escaped and who Perkin was chasing.
Emperor You mean we've recaptured them?
Guard Captain Nothing to it your 'ighness!
Emperor And the dragon was only another disguise? What luck! What an eventful day! So now ... er ... um ... let's all go back to the Palace—we'll have a trial, and we'll have some celebrations. We'll take the dragon too—that will be a surprise for the Empress. Sir Perkin, *you* escort the Princess, I shall lead the way.

The Emperor leads the way through the audience. Unfortunately for him Sophie was standing on the end of his blanket, so he walks a fair distance in his underwear—the rest of the procession, laughing, follow him—Sophie waving his blanket;—he might realise his mistake half way down the aisle

Oh dear ... oh no! ... this would happen again ... oh, and everyone is looking ... oh, how very embarrassing ... oh dear!

Everyone exits

ACT III

The Town Crier appears at the main entrance to the theatre. He rings his bell

Town Crier Oyez! Oyez! (*Ringing his bell*) Oyez! Be upstanding for His Majesty the Emperor Sigismund the Fourteenth, Lord of the Lands West of the Tarsus River. (*He moves to a central position in the theatre, ringing his bell*) Oyez! Oyez! (*Ringing his bell*) Oyez! Be upstanding for His Majesty the Emperor Sigismund the Fourteenth, Lord of the Lands West of the Tarsus River. (*He rings his bell*)

Procession enters. The Emperor first, wrapped in his blanket, then Sophie and Perkin, the Guard Captain and the Chief Minister, the dragon—Sly and Tinker, and Two Soldiers inside—Wat, and any remaining soldiers. Wat carries all equipment. As the procession enters, the Empress and her court appear on the acting area and reset the original palace scene

Empress (*advancing to meet her husband*) And just what sort of an entrance is this, Sigismund? Where are your clothes? What is all this rabble? And what is that disgusting animal that you appear to have brought home with you?

Emperor Ah well ... you see my dear ... I ... er ... lost my clothes in the ... er ... river. The dragon is a disguise hiding the two thieves ... we've recaptured them ... and Perkin here saved my life ... this is our daughter ... Sophie ... and ...

Empress Sophie! Is it really you?

Sophie Yes, mother!

Empress Go and change at once, I can't imagine what made you put on those ghastly clothes ... away with you!

Sophie Yes, Mother!

Sophie exits

Empress And now ... let's see if your word can be trusted, Sigismund ... the Guard Captain will release the prisoners and sit them over here for trial ... put a guard on them. You there ... Perkin, the odd-job man, you and your ex-pastrycook friend will go over here.

Chief Minister Mmmnmmm! (But he's a knight now.)

Empress Yes, you can stand with them, Chief Minister. And you, Sigismund, go and put some clothes on for goodness sake. Now, all of you to your places.

She claps her hands and the courtroom is set up ready for the trial. Stage right the prisoners and guard and Guard Captain. Stage left Perkin, Wat and the Chief Minister. The Empress and her attendants centre back

Wat Perkin ... could I have a word with you.
Perkin Of course ... about what, Wat?
Wat Well, I know I've let you down on two occasions—letting those prisoners go—by accident of course but ...
Perkin Yes?
Wat Well I'd like to know there *is* a reason—you see two men keep appearing and promising that if I count up to ...
Perkin Sssh! Not now, Wat, later—the trial is about to begin.
Wat But ...
Perkin Later!
Empress You can put the dragon-skin there, it may be needed as evidence. Read the charge.
Town Crier (*appearing centre, acting area*) Oyez! Oyez! All people in court today should keep silence in the presence of the Grand Judge, his esteemed Majesty the Emperor Sigismund the ...

Cue for the Emperor's entrance—if he is not ready the Town Crier should repeat this until he can make his entrance on time—it should be played to by the cast, and the Emperor should aim to miss his entrance at least once

Emperor enters

Emperor Here I am ... am I on time ... my dear?
Empress Sshh! ... carry on.
Town Crier ... the Fourteenth, Lord of the Lands West of the Tarsus River. (*He rings his bell*) The court is now in session. (*He rings his bell*)
Emperor (*about to speak*) Er ...
Empress Prisoners stand forth.

Sly and Tinker stand

Read the charge.
Town Crier You are hereby charged with knavery and trickery in that on the twenty-first day of November last, you did cause his Royal Highness the Emperor, Sigismund the Fourteenth, Lord of the Lands West of the Tarsus River to wear a non-existent suit of clothes and to consequently become a laughing stock among his subjects when he walked through the streets.
Empress In his vest and pants.
Emperor Oh, please my dear ... not again ... I mean the embarrassment ... oh really!
Town Crier (*ringing his bell*) Prisoners, how do you plead—guilty or not guilty?
Sly Not guilty. (*He nudges Tinker*)
Tinker Oh yes! Not guilty.
Empress And who appears for you?
Sly We will conduct our own defence, your highness.
Tinker We will?
Sly We will.
Empress Very well—carry on!

Act III

Sly Let the suit of clothes concerned be shown in court.
Empress What?
Sly The suit we made for the Emperor—let it be brought.
Emperor Ah but ... you see ... there is no suit ... of ...
Empress Quiet! Sigismund! Let the suit be brought!
Wat Perkin ... I ... could ... I ...

A Lady-in-waiting complies

Perkin Ssh! Later ... later!
Sly Thank you, your highness, you are so charming and gracious.
Tinker As ever!
Sly And so very handsome and elegant!
Tinker Indeed you are.
Empress Oh! Do you really think so.
Sly Quite exquisite.
Tinker Endearing.
Sly Quite so.

The suit—an empty hanger—is brought on and given to the Emperor

Wat Perkin, if I could just explain ...
Perkin Later ... sssh!
Empress Well, well how very kind.
Emperor My dear ...
Empress Just a moment, Sigismund, just a moment ... *do* carry on.
Sly Someone of your exquisite beauty ...
Empress ... Oh ...
Sly Can see the beauty in all things beautiful.
Tinker Can see the richness in all things of quality.
Sly Is not tricked by what lesser people may say.
Empress Quite ... oh yes ... quite.
Emperor My dear ... er ... the suit.

Sly takes it

Sly Now someone with no charm, no grace, no intelligence might say that a suit such as this one here was ... invisible.
Tinker But ...
Sly To someone of beauty, with grace, and with intelligence—the splendour of the cloth of gold shines forth, the sparkle of the emerald cuffs, the rubies on the collar glow in her eyes ... do you not see them ... your highness.
Empress Well ... I ...
Tinker If you are plain.
Sly If you are common, then you see ... nothing. But someone of quality and ... beauty like yourself sees the exquisite cut, the rich materials—the wealth of embroidery ... do you not see it your highness ...
Empress I do ... I do ... I believe I do ... yes the riches ... the glorious reds.
Sly Blues.

Empress I meant blues—the light is so deceptive in here.
Sly Quite so.
Tinker Indeed yes.
Empress What a suit! What workmanship! It can be seen only by people of quality and taste, intelligence and beauty ... do you see it now Sigismund?
Emperor Er ... well my dear ... I must say ... that ...
Empress Of course you do ... Chief Minister?
Chief Minister Mmmmm! (No!)
Empress I knew you would ... Guard Captain?
Guard Captain Well now, Your Majesty, from a military viewpoint I feel I should make this observation ...
Perkin There's nothing there!

Consternation

Empress What?
Wat You're right, Perkin!
Empress What!
Wat I said he's right! Now about what I was saying ... (*He moves to the side and having looked carefully begins counting very quickly in tens*)
Perkin There's nothing there! You've been tricked ... again!
Empress How dare you!
Sly Have him arrested!
Tinker Beheaded!
Sly Imprisoned!
Tinker Hung!
Sly Gagged!
Tinker Quartered!
Empress Quiet! Guard Captain, arrest that ...
Perkin Your highness!
Empress Quiet I said!
Wat A hundred!
Perkin Someone as beautiful and graceful as yourself is not surely ...
Empress I said be quiet! Guard Captain ... what was that you said?
Perkin I said surely someone as graceful and beautiful as yourself is surely not going to be taken in by such trickery?
Empress Trickery?
Perkin What they are saying is not the whole truth.
Sly But it is, your highness.
Tinker Your Majesty.
Empress I ... er ... who am I to believe?
Sly
Tinker } (*together*) Us Your Majesty.
Wat Two hundred!
Empress (*to Perkin*) Well?
Perkin What more can I say Your Majesty (*he is lost, too*) ... (*inspiration*) only a true Empress worthy of her position on the throne would be able to see that their whole argument was a pack of lies.

Act III

Empress . . . a true Empress . . .
Sly No! No! Listen your highness . . .
Tinker Your most beautiful highness . . .
Empress . . . a true Empress.
Sly Your Majesty, I would just like to . . .
Empress Imprison those men! There's nothing there!

Sophie enters

Sophie There's nothing there at all!
Emperor Nothing!
Wat Three hundred!
Guard Captain There never was anything there!
Chief Minister Mmmnn! (*I knew that too*)
Perkin Well done, Your Majesties.

Ad-libs all round

Wat Four hundred!
Town Crier (*ringing his bell*) Be it known that Sly and Tinker are hereby sentenced to five years' . . .
Empress Seven.
Emperor Fifteen.
Guard Captain Twenty-five.
Wat Four hundred and fifty.
Town Crier . . . year's labour in the Palace Kitchens! And all their monies be confiscated!

Applause. Sly and Tinker, protesting, have their purses taken from them by the Guard Captain

Sly and Tinker are marched off, protesting, by the Guard Captain. As he goes he gives Wat the purses

Wat Five hundred! (*He opens his eyes and sees the purses and rattles them*)—it was true! It was true! At last! At last!
Town Crier (*Rings bell*) Pray silence for His Majesty Emperor Sigismund . . .
Wat At last! It worked! My fortune! At last, oh my goodness . . . my own shop . . . at last!

Town Crier rings his bell

I never thought it would happen . . . but at last . . . at last . . . oh ho! ho! . . . (*He becomes aware of the situation*) . . . oh! . . . Your Majesties . . . forgive me!
Emperor Er . . . yes willingly, Wat! For you did . . . er . . . help save my life . . . in a way . . . would you like your old job back in the palace kitchens?
Empress Do you think that's wise, Sigismund?
Emperor Well . . . er . . . I . . . what do you say, Wat?
Wat Well, sire, I would like my old job back—and I would like a shop of my own. Now I can have either . . . and I don't know what to choose.

(*Pause*) I know I'll go back to the Royal Kitchens, and save my money in case I'm ever dismissed again.
Emperor A good plan, Wat—off you go to the kitchens.

Wat exits

Well, that all seems very satisfactory, my dear ... a job well done I should say.
Empress Not quite, Sigismund, not quite.
Emperor Oh ... er ... is there some other matter that I've overlooked, my dear?
Empress Only the kidnapping of our daughter, that's all!
Emperor But we have her back, my dear, and I thought ...
Empress No Sigismund! We must have justice! That fellow there must be punished.
Emperor Perkin?
Empress Yes, Perkin—he was responsible for her leaving the palace.
Sophie No, Mother, you cannot blame Perkin, he did not know who I was—he thought I was a kitchen maid, he didn't realise ...
Empress That's not good enough, my dear, the fact is that he took you away from us. Sigismund do your duty!
Emperor But ... really my dear ...
Empress Sigismund!
Emperor Oh very well ... if I must. Come here a moment, Perkin, old chap ... er ...

Perkin approaches

... it appears that I have to ... er ... punish you in some way for ... er ... well ... for ...
Empress Kidnapping the Princess Sophie!
Emperor ... for ... for ... what the Empress said. Now what would you say to losing a day's wages eh?
Empress Five years imprisonment!

Consternation on stage

Sophie No, Mother ... you can't mean it!
Emperor Really, my dear, ... isn't that a bit steep? ... eh?
Chief Minister Mmmnn! (Oh come now ... !)
Town Crier Your Highness, really, this is more than ...
Empress Five years imprisonment ... at least!

Consternation on stage again

Town Crier (*ringing his bell*) Silence for His Majesty.
Emperor Oh dear ... well now ... it does seem as though ...
Empress Get on with it, Sigismund.
Emperor ... under the law of the land ... I, Emperor Sigismund the Fourteenth, Lord of the ...
Perkin Your Majesty!
Empress Don't interrupt!

Act III

Emperor Lord of the Lands West of the Tarsus River!
Perkin (*kneeling*) Your Majesty! I plead for the right of trial by combat!
Emperor What?
Perkin I plead for the right of trial by combat.
Empress Nonsense! What rubbish! Trial by combat is only allowed for Knights of the Realm.
Perkin (*rising*) But, Your Majesty, I *am* a Knight of the Realm!
Empress What?
Emperor Great heavens, that's true, I'd forgotten ... I ... er ... knighted him, my dear, on the occasion of his saving me from the dragon. He is *Sir* Perkin.
Empress Sir Perkin?
Emperor Yes, indeed, my dear ... and as such has a right to trial by combat.
Empress Sometimes Sigismund I think you make quite the wrong decisions ... fancy creating such a knight as this ... however, he will not last long ... bring in the Guard Captain.

The Guard Captain is sent for or called for

Prepare yourself, *Sir* Perkin.

The Chief Minister acts as Perkin's Second

The Guard Captain enters, kneels to the Emperor

Emperor Er ... yes ... oh dear ... Guard Captain, as my champion you must fight Sir Perkin here ... single combat ... to the ... er ... death.
Guard Captain Fight him your Highness? But ...
Empress That's right! That's right! Get on with it, Captain—get on with it?
Guard Captain But your Highness ... I ...
Empress Get on with it!

The Guard Captain goes to his place

Guard Captain Sorry about this, Perkin.
Perkin It's all right ... you've got your job to do.
Guard Captain I'm glad you understand.

They position themselves for the fight

Empress Begin!

The Town Crier rings his bell

The fight progresses. Even with a gammy leg the Guard Captain is doing well. Perkin holds his own, but gradually he loses ground. The Guard Captain knocks his sword from his hand ... he could kill him with one blow but ...

Guard Captain Oh! Oh! I've got something in my eye.

The Chief Minister helps him—the Guard Captain winks, and Perkin recovers. The fight goes on again, and again the Guard Captain knocks the sword out of Perkin's grasp ...

Empress Now you have him! Now! Now!

Guard Captain (*going to her*) What was that, your highness?

Laughter in Court as they realise what is happening, that the Guard Captain will not kill Perkin ... the fight recommences, and again the Guard Captain shows his supremacy, forcing Perkin to his knees, but ...

(*Moving away from Perkin*) ... oh, oh! ... I've got a spot of cramp in my foot ... oh! oh!

Laughter ... and the fight continues, ... Perkin gains the upper hand, and actually disarms the Guard Captain but ...

Perkin Oh, excuse me. (*He feigns a sneeze*)
Guard Captain Bless you!
Perkin Thank you very much!
Guard Captain Not at all!

The fight continues

Empress Stop! Stop! Stop!

They do

What is all this? This is no combat! You're not making any effort to harm each other—what is the reason for this—speak!

Perkin and the Guard Captain do an "after you" routine

Guard Captain Well, your highness we ... er ... that is I know this man so well ... and he did in fact ... save me too from the dragon ... and ...
Empress Well?
Guard Captain Well ... I thought that (*inspiration*) being a true Empress worthy of her position on the throne you would realise the quality of gratitude to others.
Empress What? A true Empress ... oh! ... er ... yes ... yes ... I er ... see. And you Sir Perkin?
Perkin Well, your Highness, I look upon the Captain here as a fellow knight and ... under the circumstances, your being a true Empress worthy of her position on the throne, you would realise my situation of loyalty to a fellow officer ...
Empress A true Empress ... yes ... yes ... I see that too ... what shall I do, Sigismund?
Emperor Well, my dear ... as a true Empress worthy of her position on the throne, you should pardon them both ... showing your extreme kindness and charity.
Empress Oh yes ... yes ... I see ... as a true Empress ... very well, you are both pardoned, the Captain for failing ... to ... to fight well enough, and Sir Perkin for ... for ... well for happening to be with the Princess Sophie when she ran away.
Emperor Well done, my dear! Well done!

Applause all round

And now ... let's have a celebration ... eh?

Act III 35

The Town Crier rings his bell

Empress What for, Sigismund?
Emperor Well ... er ... um ... yes ... what for I wonder?

Discussion among those on stage. Perkin and Sophie talk together

Perkin For the Royal Wedding, Your Majesties!
Empress Royal Wedding?
Emperor Royal Wedding?
Empress Between whom?
Sophie Sir Perkin and myself, Mother.

Happiness among all on stage

Empress NEVER!

Surprise

Sophie But Mother ...
Empress No! I'm adamant!
Emperor But, my dear, surely with (*he waves all closer*) your being a ...
Sophie ... true Empress worthy of ...
Town Crier her position ...
Guard Captain on the throne ...
Chief Minister Mmmnmm!
Perkin You would grant this request.
Sophie Please, Mother?

A pause

Empress A true Empress ...
All (*softly*) Yes.
Empress Worthy of her position ...
Emperor On the throne.

Pause

Empress Very well ... I agree!

Applause and cheers all round

Town Crier (*ringing his bell*) Oyez! Oyez! Oyez! The wedding of Her Royal Highness the Princess Sophie to Sir Perkin, Knight of the Lands East of the Tarsus River, is hereby announced. (*He rings the bell again*)

Wat comes in—wearing apron and hat—with Sly and Tinker carrying a large tray of freshly baked cakes

Wat Your Majesties—my first baking. Fresh from the oven. Help yourselves. Perkin, one for you? Princess Sophie?

The cakes are handed round, not to Sly and Tinker of course, who whisper together—a plan. All are about to eat ...

Sly Stop!

Tinker Do not take a single mouthful!
Sly Put them down.
Tinker Now!
Emperor What?
Wat Yes?
Empress What is this?

General ad-lib.—"what's this all about?"

Sly Your Majesties: Do not be tricked.
Tinker Take care.
Sly Suppose this pastrycook has once again put plaster of Paris in his baking.
Wat Never! Why I wouldn't ... of all the cheek ...
Empress Silence! Now what were you saying?
Sly He might well have put plaster in this batch ...
Tinker To have his revenge on you all.
Sly Plaster of Paris.
Tinker Or ...
Sly
Tinker } *(together)* Poison.
Wat It's not true, Your Majesties—I swear it.
Sly Can you be sure, your greatness?
Tinker Can you really be sure?
Wat I wouldn't, your Highness ... I really haven't ... I ...
Sly He's done it before ...
Tinker He might do it again.
Empress Speak! Pastrycook.
Wat Well ... I ... er ... how can I ... I mean what can I say to convince you ... I ...

Perkin whispers to Wat

Eh? ... oh yes ... Well, your highness, under the circumstances I thought that being ...
All (*except Tinker and Sly*) a true Empress worthy of her position on the throne ...
Wat ... you would know that I speak the truth.

A pause

Empress (*To Sly and Tinker*) I don't believe you.

Cheers all round

You have been telling lies. You will be banished from the kingdom—see to it, Guard Captain.
Guard Captain With pleasure, your 'ighness.
Empress And now to show my faith in you, Wat the Pastrycook, I will be the first to eat one of your delicious cakes.

She bites into one and chokes. There is consternation on stage! Could it really be poisoned?

Act III

Emperor My dear, are you all right?
Sophie Mother, what is it?
Perkin Your Majesty, are you well?
Empress It's ... all right ... a crumb went down the wrong way ... the cake is excellent.
All (*except Wat*) Well done Wat!
                 Good for the Pastrycook!
                 Three cheers for Wat! (*There are*)

Wat is congratulated and the cakes eaten—even the audience might have one or two. Wat is carried out in triumph

   Everyone exits

FURNITURE AND PROPERTY LIST

ACT I

Off stage: Large padlocked box **(Wat** and **Perkin)**
Large padlocked box **(Wat** and **Perkin)**
Banner **(Soldier)**
Swords, food **(Princess Sophie)**

Personal: **Town Crier:** Bell
Guard Captain: Sword
Perkin: Handkerchief

ACT II

Strike: Large padlocked boxes

Off stage: Weapons and provisions, including pack with clothes in **(Wat)**
Boots **(Wat)**
Large fish **(Wat)**
Eel **(Wat)**
Firewood **(Perkin)**
Pike draped with Emperor's wet clothes (including a blanket and cloak) **(Soldiers)**
Map **(Town Crier)**

Personal: **Town Crier:** Bell, handkerchief
Sly: Knife
Tinker: Knife
Sly and **Tinker:** gags to put on Sophie and later Wat
Perkin: Sword

ACT III

Off stage: Equipment **(Wat)**
Empty clothes' hanger **(Lady-in-Waiting)**
Large tray of cakes **(Sly and Tinker)**

Personal: **Town Crier:** Bell
Perkin: sword
Guard Captain: sword

LIGHTING PLOT

General lighting throughout play

EFFECTS PLOT

ACT I

Cue 1   **Wat** increases his speed of counting   (Page 6)
          Drum-beat or fanfare

Cue 2   **Perkin**, **Wat** and **Sophie** exit   (Page 12)
          Noise, alarm bells and shouting from Palace

ACT II

No cues

ACT III

No cues

MADE AND PRINTED IN GREAT BRITAIN BY
LATIMER TREND & COMPANY LTD PLYMOUTH
MADE IN ENGLAND